My Duluth (

Antonia Welsch

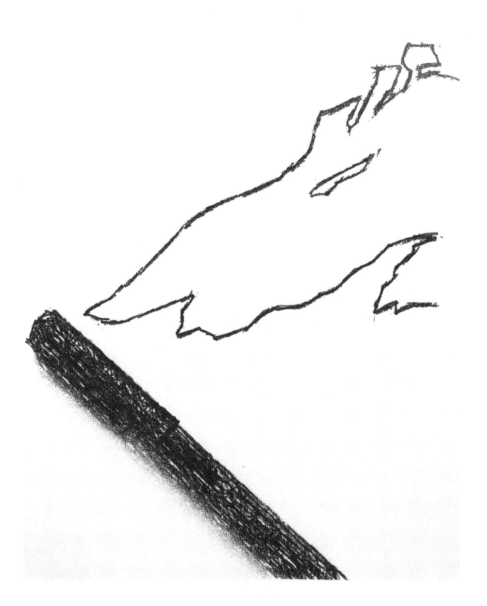

First Printing: 2020

ISBN: 978-1-79483-904-5

Inquiries and additional orders can go to www.iamantonia.com

Special discounts are available on quantity purchases by corporations, associations, educators, and others. For details, contact the author at the address listed above.

U.S. trade bookstores and wholesalers: Please contact the author using the address listed above.

For Sweet Evey

When I moved to Minnesota, I really liked it here.

NORTH

Minneapolis

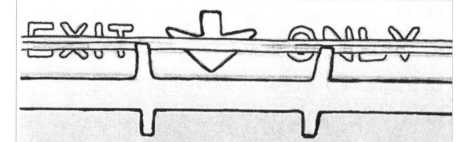

I discovered there were trails and lakes and nice people and something called "hot dish."

But soon I began hearing about a place in Minnesota I'd like more
than all the others.

A place called Duluth.

When I finally made it up north I wondered what took me so long.

There was camping.

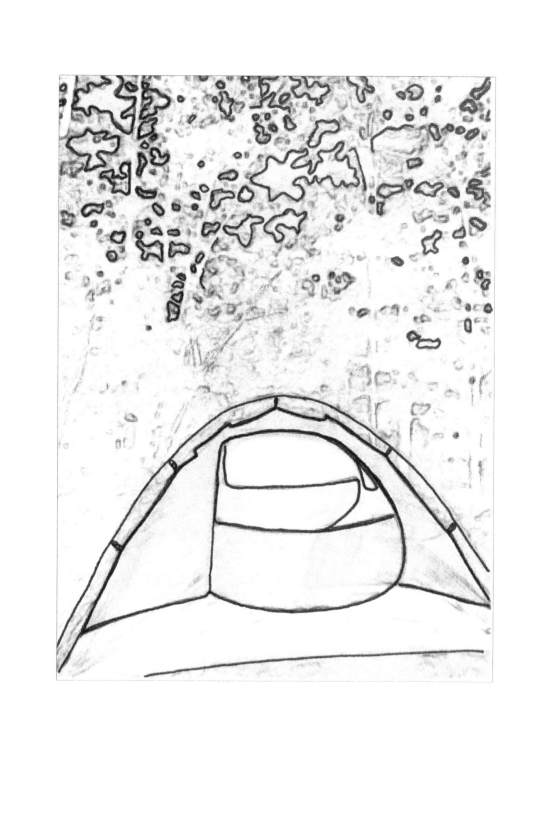

And Canal Park.

There was the Superior Hiking Trail.

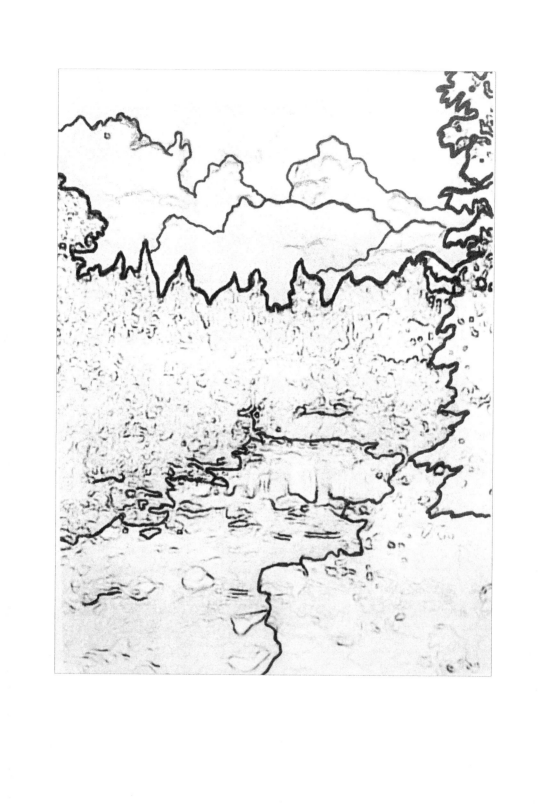

And Park Point Beach.

There was Leif Erikson Park.

And of course plenty of good food and drink.

But most impressive of all was that mighty, powerful, awe-inspiring Lake Superior.

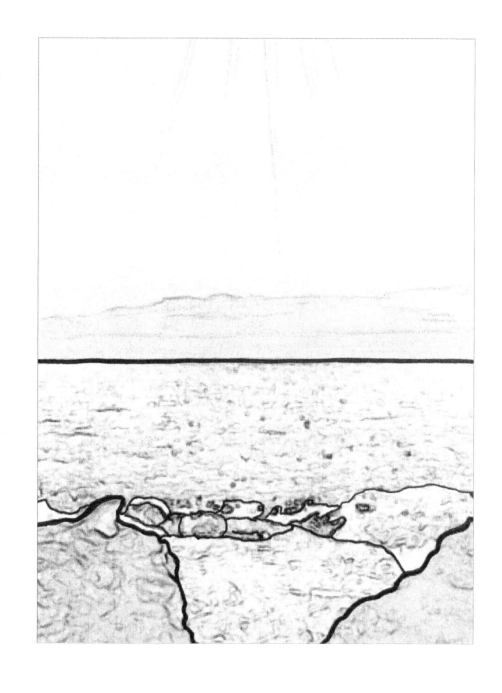

I fell in love.

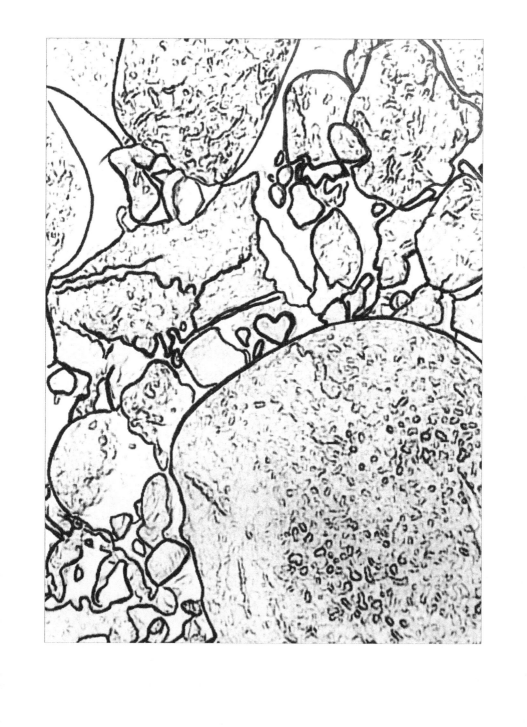

And year after year I found myself going back.

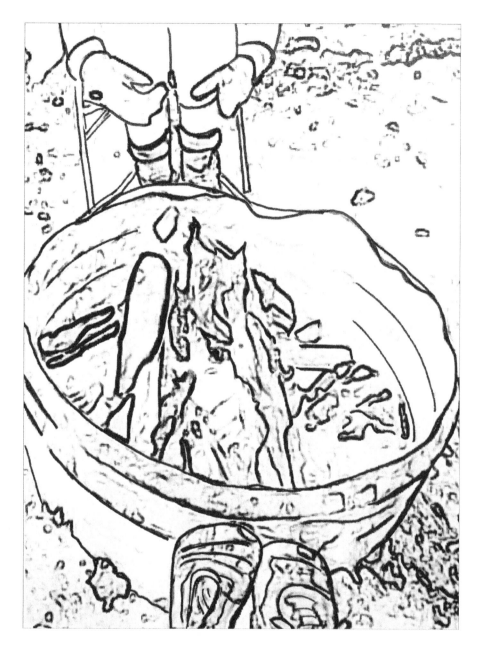

To discover new sights and sounds.

And enjoy some familiar ones too.

Sitting on the shore watching the sunrise became one of my favorite things.

And I found myself doing it again and again.

Visit after visit.

Years went by.

When I met the love of my life we got married near Two Harbors.

And it wasn't long before we were able to bring our son up north and show him all the places that were important to us.

Now he calls the Lift Bridge, "Mama's Bridge."

Instead of the peace and quiet I used to enjoy...

...there is a lot more howling at the moon and throwing sticks at the sunrise.

But that's okay, too.

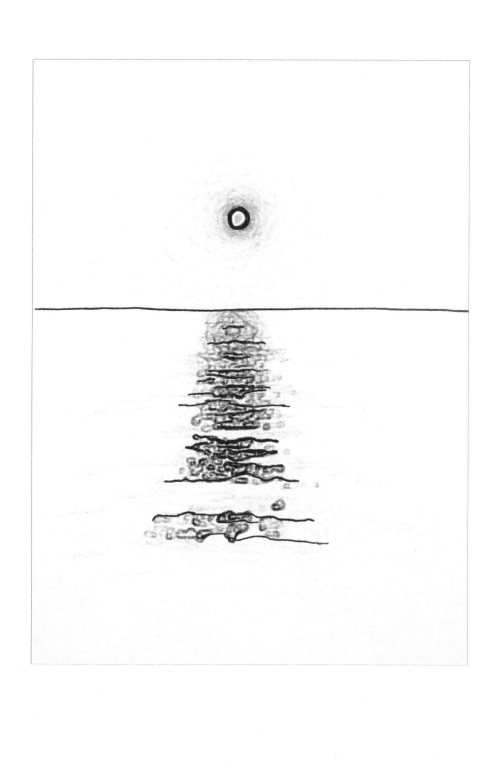

Now it's not just my happy place. It's ours.

My life has changed a lot since I moved to Minnesota.

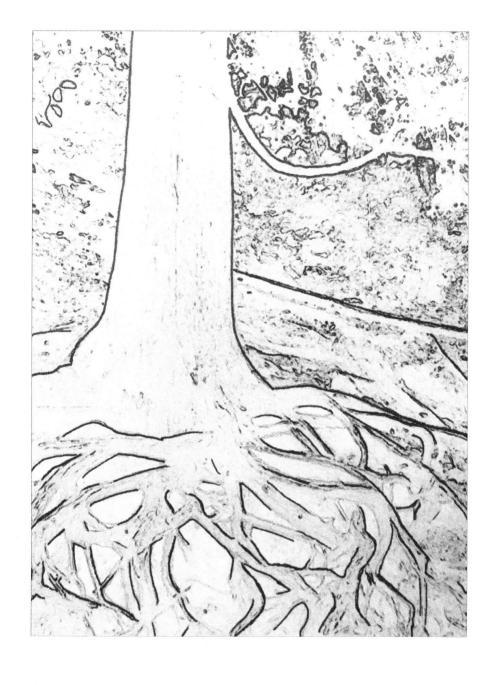

But my love of Duluth never has.

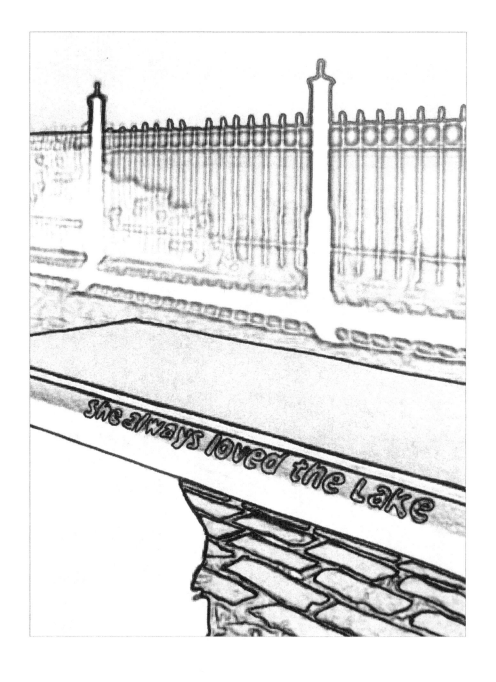

Someday I'll have a bit of land of my own...

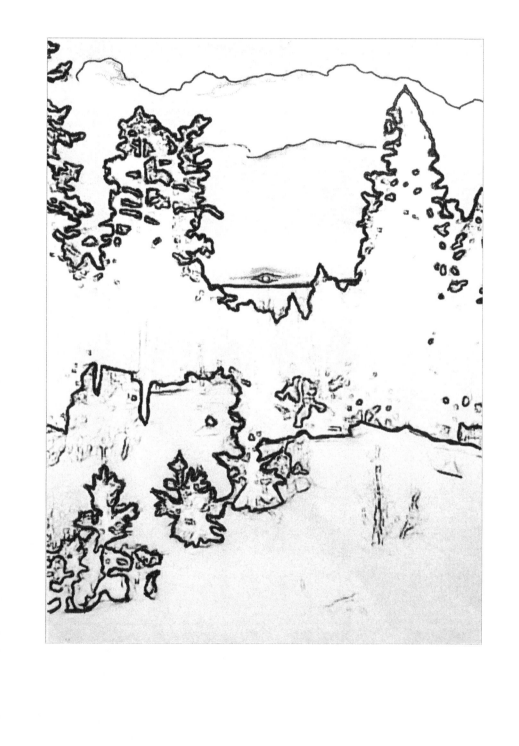

...and a cabin too.

But for now I'll color...

...and dream of my next trip up north.

What's your favorite part of Duluth?

Draw your own image here.

Antonia Welsch is a writer living in Minneapolis, Minnesota
with her husband and son. She dreams of one day living on the
north shore (somewhere between Duluth and Two Harbors).

Sometimes big dreams start with little coloring books.

Enjoy and share your pages online.
#myduluthcoloringbook

www.iamantonia.com

Made in the USA
Monee, IL
29 April 2020

28720912R00044